ALL ABOUT
REPTILES &
AMPHIBIANS

by Dee Phillips

ALL ABOUT
REPTILES &
AMPHIBIANS

Copyright © **ticktock Entertainment Ltd 2006**

First published in Great Britain in 2006 by **ticktock Media Ltd.,**

Unit 2, Orchard Business Centre, North Farm Road, Tunbridge Wells, Kent, TN2 3XF

ISBN 978 1 84696 629 3 pbk

Printed in China

Picture Credits: Alamy; 90t. OSF; 13, 15, 17, 27, 57, 79.

Every effort has been made to trace copyright holders, and we apologise in advance for any omissions. We
would be pleased to insert the appropriate acknowledgments in any subsequent edition of this publication.

CONTENTS

Words that appear in **bold** are explained in the glossary.

MEET THE REPTILES AND AMPHIBIANS

Reptiles is the word we use to describe some of the animals that live on Earth. Snakes, tortoises, turtles, lizards, crocodiles and alligators are all reptiles.

Amphibians are another group of animals.

They mostly live in or near water.

Frogs, toads, newts and salamanders

are all amphibians.

In some ways, they are very similar: their inside body temperature goes up and down with the air or water around them. Your body temperature stays the same on the inside, no matter how hot or cold it is outside.

Most reptiles and amphibians lay eggs.

But there are also differences: some amphibians lay their eggs in water or under leaves and the babies, which are called larvae or tadpoles, live and breathe under water, like fish. When they get bigger, they move onto land. Another difference is that reptiles' skin is made up of **scales**, but most amphibians have a smooth, moist, and sometimes warty skin.

A WORLD OF REPTILES AND AMPHIBIANS
The map on this page shows our world

The different parts of the world are called continents. North America and Africa are both continents. Some of the animals in this book live in lots of places on just one continent. Other animals live on many different continents.

Some animals in this book only live in one country, such as America or Japan.

When you read about an animal in your book, see if you can find the place where they live on the map.

Can you point to the part of the world where you live?

REPTILES AND AMPHIBIANS HABITATS

Some animals live in hot places, such as deserts, others live in forests or in the ocean. The different types of places where animals live are called **habitats**.

Look for these pictures in your book, and they will tell you what kind of habitat each animal lives in.

Deserts–hot, dry, sandy places where it hardly ever rains

Mountains– high, rocky places

Grasslands–dry places covered with grass

Lakes, ponds, rivers or streams

Rainforests– warm forests with lots of rain

Temperate forests– cool forests with trees that lose their leaves in winter

Oceans

Seashores

REPTILE AND AMPHIBIAN MENUS

Some reptiles and amphibians only eat meat, fish or bugs and spiders. Others only eat plants. Many reptiles and amphibians eat both meat and plants.

Look for these pictures in your book, and they will tell you what kind of food each animal eats.

Plants

Meat (other animals)

Fish

Bugs or spiders

ADDER

The adder is also known as a viper. It lives across parts of Europe and east Asia. It is the only **venomous snake** in north west Europe.

An adder's bite is rarely **fatal**. It can cause mild swelling, and is very painful, but it is unlikely to kill you.

Adders like to sunbathe. They are often seen basking on rocks.

An adder eats rats and lizards. It hunts its **prey** by chasing it or by the technique of **ambush**.

3 ft

6 ft

Adder moms only have babies every two to three years. They have litters of up to 20 young.

Adders can be gray, brown, dark red or black. Most have a zigzag line running down their back.

PYTHON

Pythons are all **snakes** which loop their bodies around their prey and squeeze to kill it. None are **venomous**.

Some can swallow a deer whole.

The reticulated python (above) is the world's longest snake, some have grown as big as 32 feet.

6 ft   12 ft   18 ft   24 ft   30 ft

There are 26 known species of python. This is a green tree python.

Python moms lay between 15 to 100 eggs. Moms keep the eggs warm with their bodies until the eggs hatch.

BOA CONSTRICTOR

Boa constrictors get their name from the way they wrap their long bodies around their **prey**. They squeeze harder and harder until the prey cannot breathe anymore, and swallow their victims whole.

Boa constrictors are excellent swimmers. They often decide to go in water to escape the heat during summer.

Dark patches of color help to hide boa constrictors when they are hunting for prey.

3 ft   6 ft   9 ft   12 ft   15 ft

Boa constrictors are very large snakes. They are adaptable creatures that can grow to frightening sizes.

ANACONDA

Anacondas live in South America.

They are the heaviest **snakes** in the world.

Some anacondas weigh 550 pounds.

Their eyes and nostrils are on top of their heads, so they can see and breathe when they are hiding in water.

Anacondas hide from their **prey** in **shallow** water.

3 ft   6 ft   9 ft   12 ft   15 ft   18 ft   21 ft   28 ft   32 ft   35 ft

Anacondas can catch big animals, such as pigs and deer and swallow them whole.

Anacondas give birth to live baby snakes. The babies can swim and hunt just a few hours after they are born.

GABOON VIPER

Gaboon vipers are a kind of **snake**. They use their special teeth, called **fangs**, to inject **venom** into their **prey**.

Gaboon vipers have the longest fangs of any venomous snake. The fangs are about as long as your finger!

Gaboon vipers hunt for frogs, birds and other small creatures.

3 ft

6 ft

Gaboon viper moms only have babies every two or three years.

They live in **forests** in Africa.

This skin pattern helps the gaboon viper to hide among leaves.

17

BLACK MAMBA

As well as being the most **venomous snake**, the black mamba is probably the fastest too.

The black mamba is not actually black, but gray or brown.

It makes its home in a rock crevice or a hollow tree.

Black mambas come out during the day and feed on birds and mammals.

3 ft   6 ft   9 ft   12 ft   15 ft

Females lay 12–17 eggs in chambers underground.

They live in east and southern Africa.

CORAL SNAKE

These **venomous**, brightly colored **snakes** live in warm parts of the Americas. There are about 40 species.

These colorful bands tell **predators** that the snake is dangerous and not good to eat.

They have smooth **scales**.

Coral snakes have a small head.

3 ft

6 ft

They eat other snakes
and small **lizards**.

These snakes spend their time hidden in
the forest and they only come out at night.

CORN SNAKE

Corn snakes live in North America. They live up trees, on buildings or on the ground, hiding under logs and rocks.

Corn snakes eat rats and mice.

They taste the air with their tongues to find out if dinner is close by.

They have a Y-shaped tongue.

3 ft   6 ft

Snakes have no eyelids so their eyes stay open even when they are asleep.

Mom corn snakes lay eggs in piles of leaves. The baby snakes **hatch** from the eggs after 60 days.

EMERALD TREE BOA

Emerald tree boas live in **rainforest** trees in South America. They kill and eat birds and small animals such as mice by crushing them.

This green skin helps the snake hide among the tree leaves.

Emerald tree boas wrap their bodies around a branch and then reach out with their heads to catch their **prey**.

3 ft   6 ft   9 ft   12 ft   15 ft

The baby boas are red, yellow or orange when they are born. They start to go green when they are about one year old, like this one.

Emerald tree boas give birth to live babies.

COBRA

Cobras are **snakes** that live in lots of different **habitats** in south east Asia and Africa. They are very **venomous**.

These markings on the back of the hood look a bit like eyes.

When the cobra meets an enemy, it rears up and spreads this hood of skin.

The spitting cobra spits venom from its **fangs**. The poison can hit **prey** 6.5 feet away.

3 ft   6 ft   9 ft   12 ft   15 ft

Cobras eat rats, birds, **lizards**, toads and other **snakes**.

Indian cobras lay about 12–20 eggs. The baby **snakes hatch** after 60 days.

SEA SNAKES

Sea **snakes** live in warm seas. They are highly **venomous**. Like land snakes, sea snakes are **scaly reptiles** who shed their skin, have forked tongues and breathe air.

Sea snakes have specialized flattened tails for swimming, and nostrils which close underwater.

They do not have gill slits and need to breathe air.

All sea snakes give birth to live young, apart from the banded sea snake which lays eggs on the shore.

3 ft   6 ft   9 ft   12 ft   15 ft

Sea snakes are usually found in **shallow** water, where they swim about the bottom feeding on fish and eels.

RATTLESNAKE

Rattlesnakes are **venomous**. They catch their **prey** by biting them with their **fangs**.

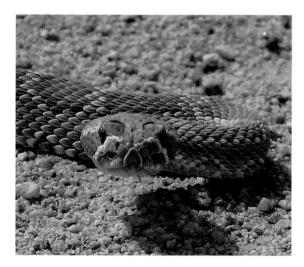

The rattle is made of hard **scales**. It sounds like dried peas in a tin.

If a rattlesnake hears a person or animal nearby, it rattles the end of its tail to say, "Go away!"

3 ft   6 ft   9 ft   12 ft

This timber rattlesnake lives in **deserts** and hot places in America. It gives birth to live babies.

Rattlesnakes hunt **lizards**, birds and small animals such as rats.

ALLIGATOR

Alligators are very big **reptiles** that spend a lot of time in the water. They float about in **lakes**, rivers and **swamps**. There are two types of alligator: American and Chinese.

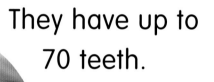

They have up to 70 teeth.

They have webbed feet for swimming.

Alligators hunt for fish, **snakes**, turtles, **lizards** and birds. They gobble up their **prey** whole.

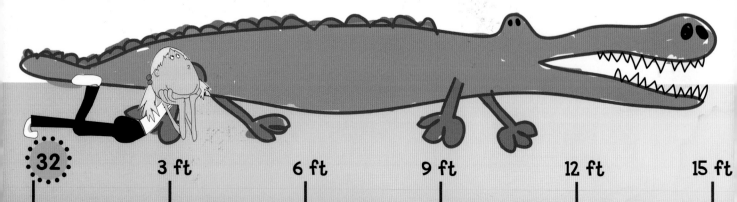

3 ft   6 ft   9 ft   12 ft   15 ft

The **hatchlings** call out "PEEP PEEP" to their mom as they **hatch**.

The mother carries the tiny hatchlings to the water inside her mouth.

CROCODILE

Crocodiles are huge **reptiles**. They are **predators**. Crocodiles live in Africa, Australia and south east Asia in **lakes**, rivers and **swamps**.

Crocodiles eat lots of fish. Sometimes they catch and eat big animals such as **buffaloes**.

Mom crocodiles lay their eggs in a hole on the sandy riverbank.

They have thick skin with **scales**.

3 ft   6 ft   9 ft   12 ft   15 ft   18 ft   21 ft   24 ft   27 ft

A crocodile egg is about twice the size of a chicken egg.

Baby crocodiles hide in their mom's mouth if there is any danger.

GHARIAL

Gharials are **reptiles** that come from the same animal family as crocodiles. They live in rivers in India and nearby countries.

Gharials have weak legs. When they are on land, they slide along on their bellies!

They have over 100 very sharp teeth in this long, thin snout.

3 ft   6 ft   9 ft   12 ft   15 ft   18 ft   21 ft   24 ft   27 f

Only boys have a
lump on their snout.

Gharials spend most of their time
in water. They mainly eat fish.

Mom gharials dig nest holes
away from the river. Then they
lay about 60 eggs in one go.

CAIMAN

This fierce **reptile** is another member of the crocodile family. Caimans live in Central and South America.

Mom caimans build a nest for their eggs made from leaves and plants. The nest is made either at the edge of the water or floating on the water.

They hunt at night for fish, other **reptiles**, birds and **amphibians**.

3 ft   6 ft   9 ft   12 ft   15 ft

Sometimes caimans share a nest.
The moms work as a team guarding
the nest against **predators**.

GECKO

Geckos live in warm places like **rainforests** and **deserts**. They are the only lizards that have a voice, which sounds like "gecko". This is how they got their name.

These feet can climb anything—even, smooth, slippery glass.

There are about 400 species of gecko. The largest is a tokay (like the one above).

3 in   7 in   10 in   13 in   15 in   18 in

Geckos hunt at night for insects, but they also eat young birds, eggs and tiny mammals.

This is a Madagascan day gecko.

Most mom geckos lay eggs with soft shells. It takes up to 60 days for the eggs to **hatch**.

CHAMELEON

Chameleons are **lizards** with special skin that can change color if they get angry or excited, and can allow them to blend in with their environment.

Its tongue shoots out so fast, you cannot see it.
It is longer than the chameleon's body.

This tail can hold onto branches.

3 in   7 in   10 in   13 in   15 in   18 in

This is a Jackson's chameleon. It lives in east Africa and Hawaii.

One eye can look forwards, while the other eye is looking backwards.

IGUANA

Iguanas are a kind of large **lizard**. They live in the **rainforests**, **deserts** and one type lives by the sea.

Iguanas vary in color from green to brown to yellow.

If attacked, the iguana uses its tail like a whip.

They use their powerful legs to swim and climb trees.

3 ft

6 ft

A female iguana will dig a **shallow** trench in moist soil in which she will lay 20-70 eggs and cover the eggs with soil.

Iguanas mainly eat plants, insects, worms and small animals.

BEARDED DRAGON

The bearded dragon is a kind of **lizard**. It lives in **forests** and hot, dry places in Australia.

A frill of skin a bit like a beard.

If a **predator** comes near, the dragon puffs up its beard and opens its mouth wide to look scary.

3 ft

6 ft

They sit on branches, or sometimes on fences, keeping watch over their **territory**.

Bearded dragons eat bugs, plants, fruit and flowers. They live on the ground and in trees.

Moms lay their eggs in sandy ground. The babies **hatch** out on their own.

FRILLED LIZARD

Frilled **lizards** live in **forests** in Australia. They live up in the trees, but search for food on the ground.

Frilled lizards eat bugs and other smaller lizards.

When a **predator** comes close, the frilled lizard opens up its big frill of skin and hisses to make itself seem scary. Then it quickly runs up a tree to escape.

7 in   14 in   21 in   28 in   35 in

The frill folds down over the lizard's shoulders.

Mom frilled lizards lay about eight eggs at a time.

THORNY DEVIL LIZARD

Thorny devils are **lizards** that live in hot **deserts** in Australia. They are strange, shy creatures.

The thorny devil lizard has spikes all over its body. The spikes protect it from **predators**.

7 in   14 in   21 in   28 in   35 in

Thorny devils eat ants. They lick them up with their tongues— one ant at a time.

They eat thousands of ants in one meal, so dinner takes a long time.

Mom thorny devil lizards lay their eggs in underground **burrows**.

THAI WATER DRAGON

Thai water dragons are **lizards** that live in south east Asia. They live in **forests** near **lakes** and streams.

If a **predator** comes close, the lizard escapes into the water. The tail helps the lizard move through water.

Thai water dragons spend time on the ground and in trees.

Their long toes with claws are good for climbing.

3 ft   6 ft   9 ft   12 ft   15 ft

Moms lay eggs in **burrows** and cover them with earth and leaves.

Thai water dragons eat small animals, such as other lizards. Sometimes they eat plants.

BLUE-TONGUED SKINK

This large **lizard** lives in various different **habitats** in Australia.

It has a wide head.

It has a chubby body.

It has short legs.

In the daytime, the blue-tongued skink sunbathes and looks for snails, bugs, fruit, flowers and berries to eat.

Baby skinks are three inches long when they are born.

3 ft

6 ft

If a **predator** attacks, the skink hisses and rolls out its long, bright blue tongue to scare away the other animal.

At night, it sleeps in a log or pile of dead leaves.

GILA MONSTER

Gila monsters are big, **venomous**, slow-moving **lizards**. They live in **deserts** in North America and Mexico.

They have scaly skin that looks like small beads.

Gila monsters store fat in their tails. Their bodies use the fat for energy when there is no food available.

Gila monsters eat rats, birds, frogs, other lizards and eggs.

When they bite their **prey**, venom comes out of their teeth.

7 in   14 in   21 in   28 in   35 in

Baby gila monsters are over three inches long when they **hatch** from their eggs.

KOMODO DRAGON

The giant Komodo dragon is the biggest of all the **lizards**. Komodo dragons live on **islands** near south east Asia.

They can smell food from up to six miles away and often eat other animals' leftover meat.

The Komodo has a deadly bite from the **poisonous** bacteria in its saliva.

They have a forked tongue.

3 ft   6 ft   9 ft   12 ft   15 ft

Mom dragons dig out large **burrows** in sandy ground for their eggs.

When the babies **hatch**, they live up in the trees to stay away from **predators**.

SLOW WORM

Slow worms look like **snakes** but they are actually **lizards** with no legs. (Lizards have eyelids; snakes do not). When it is cold in winter, slow worms **hibernate**.

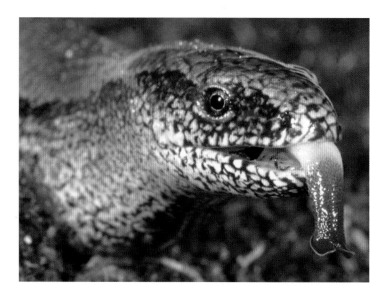

They eat bugs, worms and slugs.

Slow worms live in fields and on farmland across Europe and west Asia.

7 in   14 in   21 in   28 in   35 in

If a **predator** grabs a slow worm's tail, it breaks off. But it will soon grow back.

Mom slow worms give birth to live babies.

TUATARA

The tuatara looks like a **lizard**, but is not. They are found on two small groups of islands off the coast of New Zealand.

Tuatara eggs take up to a year to develop inside the female's body and take up to 14 months to **hatch**.

Tuataras live a very long time (possibly over 100 years).

3 ft

6 ft

They live in burrows and
mainly come out at night.

They eat beetles, crickets, small **lizards**
and occasionally eggs and chicks of birds.

GALAPAGOS TORTOISE

Tortoises are reptiles with shells. Galapagos tortoises are the biggest tortoises in the world. They live on **islands** near South America.

They like to munch on plants, grass and **cacti**. They also like to sunbathe and relax in muddy puddles.

Like other tortoises, they can pull their limbs and head inside their shell.

3 ft   6 ft   9 ft   12 ft   15 ft

Moms dig a nest in sandy ground. They lay eggs the size of tennis balls.

Tortoises are related to turtles, who live in the ocean, and terrapins, who live in freshwater.

SEA TURTLE

Sea turtles are swimming **reptiles** with shells. There are many different types of sea turtle and they live in oceans all around the world.

Most sea turtles eat meat, but the green turtle, like this one, lives on plants.

All sea turtle species are endangered or threatened.

3 ft   6 ft   9 ft

Mom turtles crawl up on to a beach and dig a hole in the sand for their eggs.

When the eggs **hatch**, the baby turtles have to run to the sea before they are spotted by **predators**.

67

SNAPPING TURTLE

This fierce **reptile** lives in **lakes**, ponds, streams and rivers in parts of North and South America.

The snapping turtle has no teeth. It uses its hard, hooky beak to slice at **prey**.

The turtle's head cannot fit into its shell so it bites at **predators** to protect itself.

Moms dig nest holes on land with their back legs. They lay 20–30 eggs, then go back to their pond or river.

7 in   14 in   21 in   28 in   35 in

Snapping turtles eat frogs, toads, **snakes**, small animals and plants.

They hide, buried in underwater mud, ready to jump out on their prey.

TERRAPINS

Terrapins are freshwater turtles that live in swampy waters, **lakes** and rivers. They spend much of their lives in the water.

This is a helmeted terrapin. Like all terrapins, it eats meat and catches most of its **prey** in the water.

Some terrapins can spend the winter underwater, buried in mud.

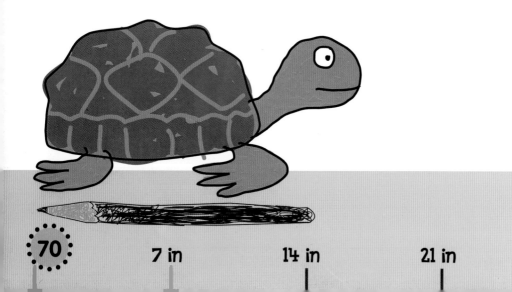

7 in   14 in   21 in   28 in   35 in

Terrapins, like this diamondback terrapin, lay eggs on land, cover them up, and then leave the **hatchlings** to fend for themselves.

They eat fish, water insects, insect **larvae** and snails.

PAINTED TURTLE

The painted turtle lives in North America, and it is also called a painted terrapin. It spends most of its time in the water, but suns itself while lying on a rock, on a log or the shore.

They live in ponds, **lakes**, marshes and slow-moving rivers.

In the wild, they can live between 5–10 years.

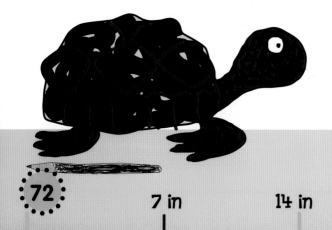

7 in   14 in   21 in   28 in   35 in

During very cold weather, northern painted turtles **hibernate** by burying themselves in the mud.

Female painted turtles lay 5–10 eggs in a shallow pit that they dig with their hind legs. They then abandon them, and the eggs **hatch** in about 10–11 weeks.

EUROPEAN COMMON FROG

The European common frog is the most common frog in northern Europe. It lives close to **lakes**, ponds, rivers and streams.

Frog moms lay thousands of eggs in one go. The eggs are called frogspawn. They look like a big clump of jelly.

The baby frogs are called tadpoles. They can hatch after about two weeks, if the weather is warm enough.

7 in   14 in   21 in   28 in   35 in

Frogs catch bugs to eat on their long, sticky tongues.

They spend most of their lives on land, and return to the water to breed.

TREEFROG

Treefrogs live in Australia, New Guinea, Europe, America and Asia. There are many different types of treefrogs.

Treefrogs have sticky pads on their fingers and toes to help them climb trees, like this red-eyed treefrog.

These frogs usually come out at night looking for bugs to eat

7 in   14 in   21 in   28 in   35 in

Giant tree frogs are the largest type of treefrog. They can grow to about four inches.

Mom frogs lay their eggs in water—the White's treefrog lays up to 3,000 eggs in one go.

HORNED FROG

There are many types of horned frog. This large, fat species lives in the rainforest in South America and Asia.

The Asian horned frog has a huge head, with two horn-like protrusions above its eyes which deter **predators**.

Females can lay up to 1,000 eggs. They wrap these around water plants.

7 in   14 in   21 in   28 in   35 in

Horned frogs catch lizards, mice and other frogs by burying themselves in the ground and pouncing as they pass by.

This is a Chacoan horned frog.

NORTH AMERICAN BULLFROG

North American bullfrogs are big, greedy frogs that live in America.

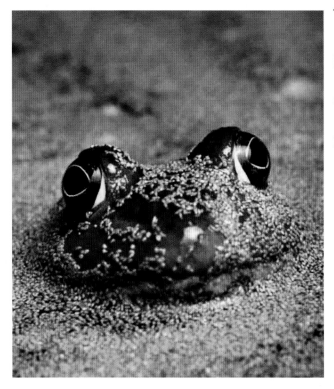

They eat other frogs, **reptiles**, birds, fish—anything they can swallow.

Bullfrogs live in **lakes**, ponds and streams.

They can leap 6 feet with their long, strong back legs.

7 in   14 in   21 in   28 in   35 in

The round circles behind the eyes are the frog's eardrums.

Dad bullfrogs protect their **territory** from other frogs by chasing them, having wrestling fights and making loud noises.

POISON DART FROG

Poison dart frogs live in **rainforests** in Central America. Native people use their poison on arrows and darts when they go hunting.

When the eggs hatch, they carry the tadpoles on their backs to tree holes filled with water.

Poison dart frogs can be red, blue or green.

Green poison dart frog moms lay 5–13 eggs in water-filled tree holes.

7 in   14 in   21 in   28 in   35 in

The bright colors are a defense mechanism. They warn **predators** that the frog is **poisonous.**

EUROPEAN COMMON TOAD

The European common toad is one of Europe's most common amphibians. It also lives in Europe and parts of Asia and Africa.

They spend the day in cool, damp places. They mainly come out at night, looking for bugs and slugs to eat.

Mom toads lay long strings of eggs in ponds.

7 in   14 in   21 in   28 in   35 in

Toads have special places behind their eyes which make nasty-tasting stuff that stops **predators** eating them.

FIRE SALAMANDER

The fire salamander is an **amphibian**. It lives in **forests** in Africa, Europe and west Asia.

This yellow and black skin tells **predators** that the salamander has **poison** on its skin and is bad to eat.

When they grow up, they live on land and breathe air like humans.

7 in   14 in   21 in   28 in   35 in

Fire salamanders
eat worms, slugs
and bugs.

Baby fire salamanders are called **larvae**.
They live in ponds and streams and can
breathe underwater just like fish.

JAPANESE GIANT SALAMANDER

Japanese giant salamanders are the biggest **amphibians** in the world.

They live in cold **mountain** streams and rivers in Japan.

Japanese giant salamanders eat many different foods, including crabs, bugs, mice and fish.

They can go for weeks without eating if there is no food.

3 ft

6 ft

Moms lay about 500 eggs in strings, in a hole dug by dads.

Dads guard the eggs until they **hatch**. They are very fierce if **predators** come near the eggs.

MUDPUPPY

Mudpuppies are a type of salamander. They live in freshwater, in southern Canada, central and eastern USA.

The mudpuppy has two pairs of limbs, each with a four-toed foot.

Female mudpuppies dig a nest under rocks and logs and guard their eggs until they **hatch**, about two months later.

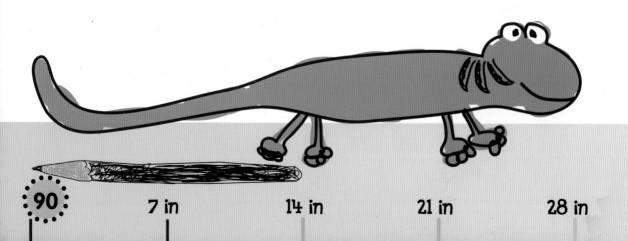

7 in   14 in   21 in   28 in   35 in

Mudpuppies have feathery, external gills.

They are brown, gray or black, usually with black spots or blotches.

GREAT CRESTED NEWT

Newts look like **lizards**, but they are **amphibians**. Great crested newts live near ponds and **lakes**, in Europe. Adult newts spend the summer or entire year in water.

In the daytime they hide under logs or stones. At night they look for food— tadpoles, worms and bug **larvae**.

Male great crested newts have a jagged crest.

7 in   14 in   21 in   28 in   35 in

Mom newts lay two to three eggs every day for about five months.

They wrap their eggs in leaves and hide them among water plants.

The **larvae hatch** out and live in the water until they become grown-ups.

Glossary

ambush A surprise attack by someone or something lying in a hidden position

amphibians Animals that spend part of their time in water and part on land; some amphibians lay their eggs in water. Frogs, toads, newts and salamanders are amphibians

bark The tough, outer covering of tree trunks and tree branches

buffaloes Big, plant-eating wild animals that look a bit like cows. Buffaloes can be over six feet tall

burrows Holes or tunnels that animals dig as homes

cacti Plants that have spikes instead of leaves; they often live in hot dry places such as deserts

deserts Places where hardly any rain falls; many lizards and snakes live in deserts, even though they are hot, dry places

fangs Very sharp teeth; snakes' fangs are hollow (like drinking straws) and are used to inject venom into their prey

fatal Causing death

forests Places where there are lots of trees

geckos Small reptiles with four legs and a tail; they are a kind of lizard; they have special feet that help them to climb up slippery things like glass

grasslands Dry places covered with grass, with very few bushes or trees

habitats Different types of places around the world, such as forests, deserts and grasslands

hatch To be born by breaking out of an egg

hatchlings The name for the babies of some reptiles; they are called hatchlings because they hatch from eggs

hibernate To spend the winter sleeping in a burrow (or other warm, safe place) while there is not much food around

lakes Large areas of inland water

islands Small areas of land completely surrounded by ocean

larvae The name for the babies of creatures such as bugs and newts; these animals start as eggs; they hatch out as larvae and then grow and change into grown-ups

lizards Reptiles with scaly skin and legs; some

lizards are tiny, while others such as the Komodo dragon (see page 58) are huge

mountains Large, rocky areas of land that are much higher than the surrounding area

poison Nasty stuff that can make a person or animal very ill and even kill them; some animals have poison inside their bodies that they use for killing their prey

poisonous The word we use to describe something that can kill when eaten

predators Animals that live by hunting and eating other animals

prey An animal that is hunted by another animal for food

rainforests Warm, jungle-like forests with very tall trees and lots of plants and animals

reptiles Animals such as snakes, lizards, tortoises and turtles. They often have scaly skin. Some reptiles lay eggs and some give birth to live babies

scales Tough, flat sections of skin on the bodies of reptiles. They are made of the same stuff as your fingernails and toenails

sea sponges Very simple ocean animals; they live attached to something such as a rock on the seabed; you might have some soft, yellow, natural sea sponge in your bathroom

shallow When something, such as water, is not very deep

snakes Long, thin reptiles with scaly skin and no legs

swamps Places where there is lots of water or mud, and the ground is soft, wet and very squishy

territory The area where an animal lives; animals guard their territories to stop other animals eating the food in the territory or taking the good places to sleep

venomous Producing a poisonous fluid injected by a bite or sting

Index